Car Classics

Compiled by Lynn Thomas
Copyright 2021, All Rights Reserved.

Dedicated to my Dad, who has been a Motörhead (car enthusiast) his whole life, and influenced me and my siblings from a very young age to distinguish cars by the sound of their engines, screaming around the race track. And at one point, he raced cars, and at another point, owned his own Rolls Royce dealership. Thank you, Dad, for everything you added to enrich my life with wonderful experiences growing up.

****

****

There is a wide variety of different cars in this book, both classic and modern, and even a fantasy image or two. It's just the love of automobiles, and even motorcycles that drives the idea of a coloring book that people can enjoy coloring, and perhaps framing and placing in a man cave or behind a bar, or giving to someone you love who appreciates cars, as a special personalized gift.

The grayscales provide you with the basis for your painting, and you chose how to fill the rest in.

There are many youtube videos available for you to learn how to do grayscale coloring. If you are challenge, go to youtube and search for what your issue is, and you're sure to find some tutorials.

And, you're invited to join my facebook group "Creative Studio Designs."

https://www.facebook.com/groups/creativestudiodesigns

We're building a group of Grayscale Colorists who appreciate high quality images. Once there, I welcome your feedback on the kinds of books you'd like to see from me in the future. And if you have questions, please ask them, we have a wonderful community of colorists of all skill levels and a wide variety of experience, who will encourage and help you along your journey.

And, if you prefer to print out your own images on your own paper, you can obtain copies of my books in pdf form on Etsy. My shop is also titled "Creative Studio Designs."

Here is the link to my Etsy Shop: https://etsy.me/38bQbby

And if you want to see the color images of these pictures, go to the flip book at https://bit.ly/3amD2OY

My hope is that my books will provide you many hours of creative coloring and soul nurturing moments, and gives you beautiful art as a result.

Happy coloring!

Lynn Thomas

I want to thank my colorist team who have all been utterly fantastic. And here are the credits to the talented colorists who colored the images on the cover.

On the Front Cover from left to right starting at the top:

1-Jaguar-Simon Amey
2-Rolls-Magriet Bester
3-Black Mustang-Magriet Bester
4-Red Pontiac-Leanne Diprose
5-Racing-Sylvie St-Onge

On the Back Cover left to right starting at the top:
7-Ford -Sandy Newman
8-Cabrio-Stephanie Frisch
9-Porsche-Simon Amey
10- Stargate-Sandy Newman

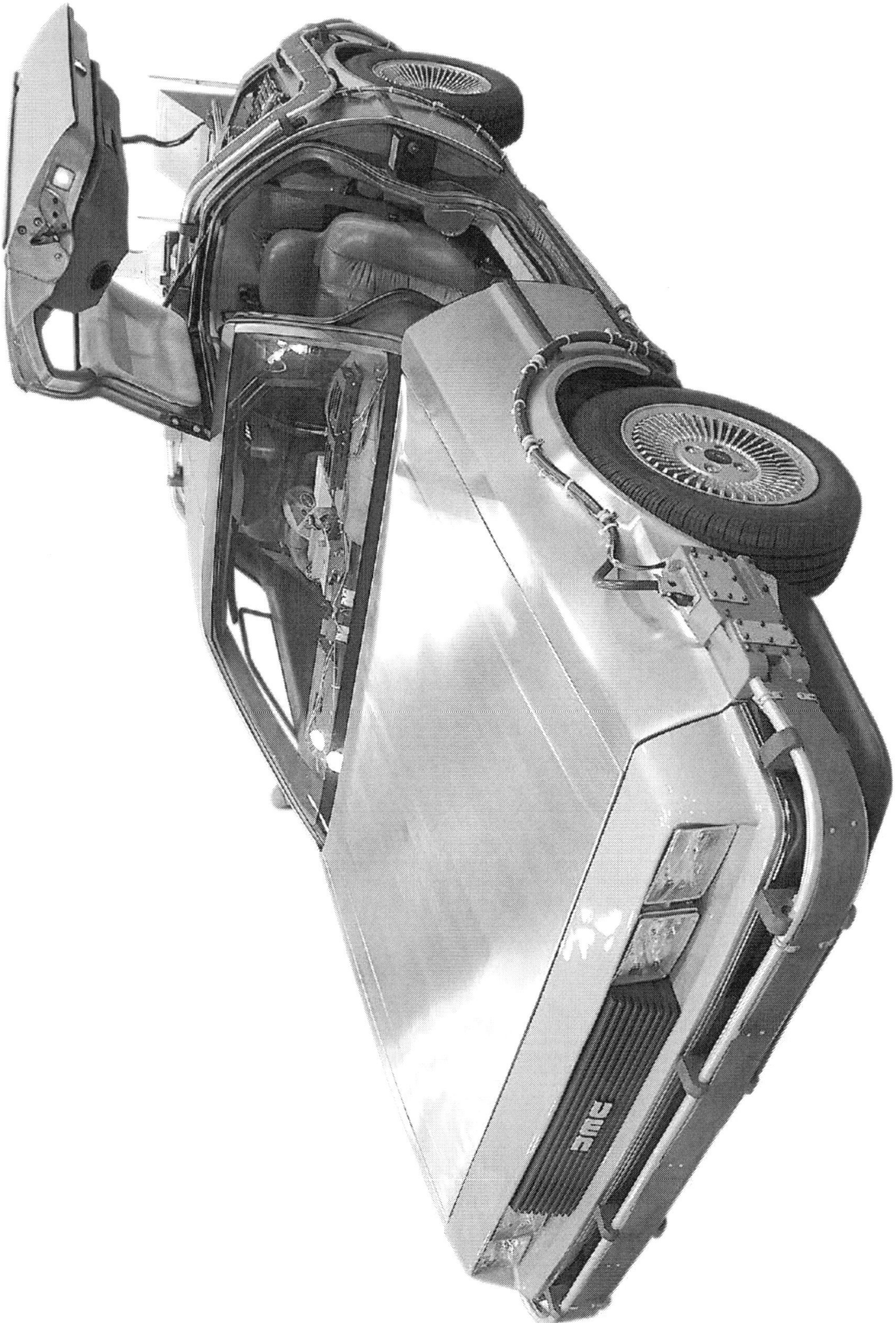

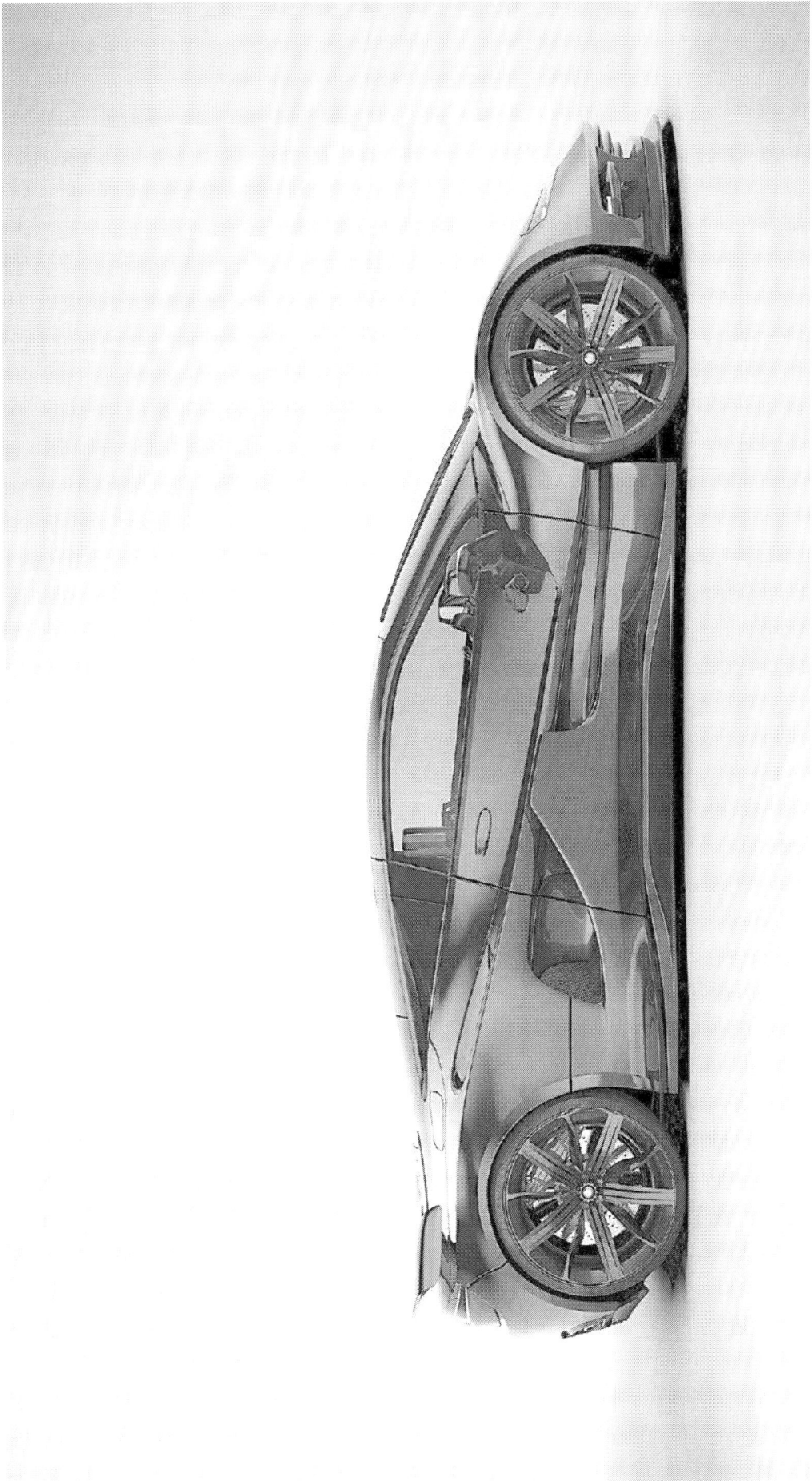

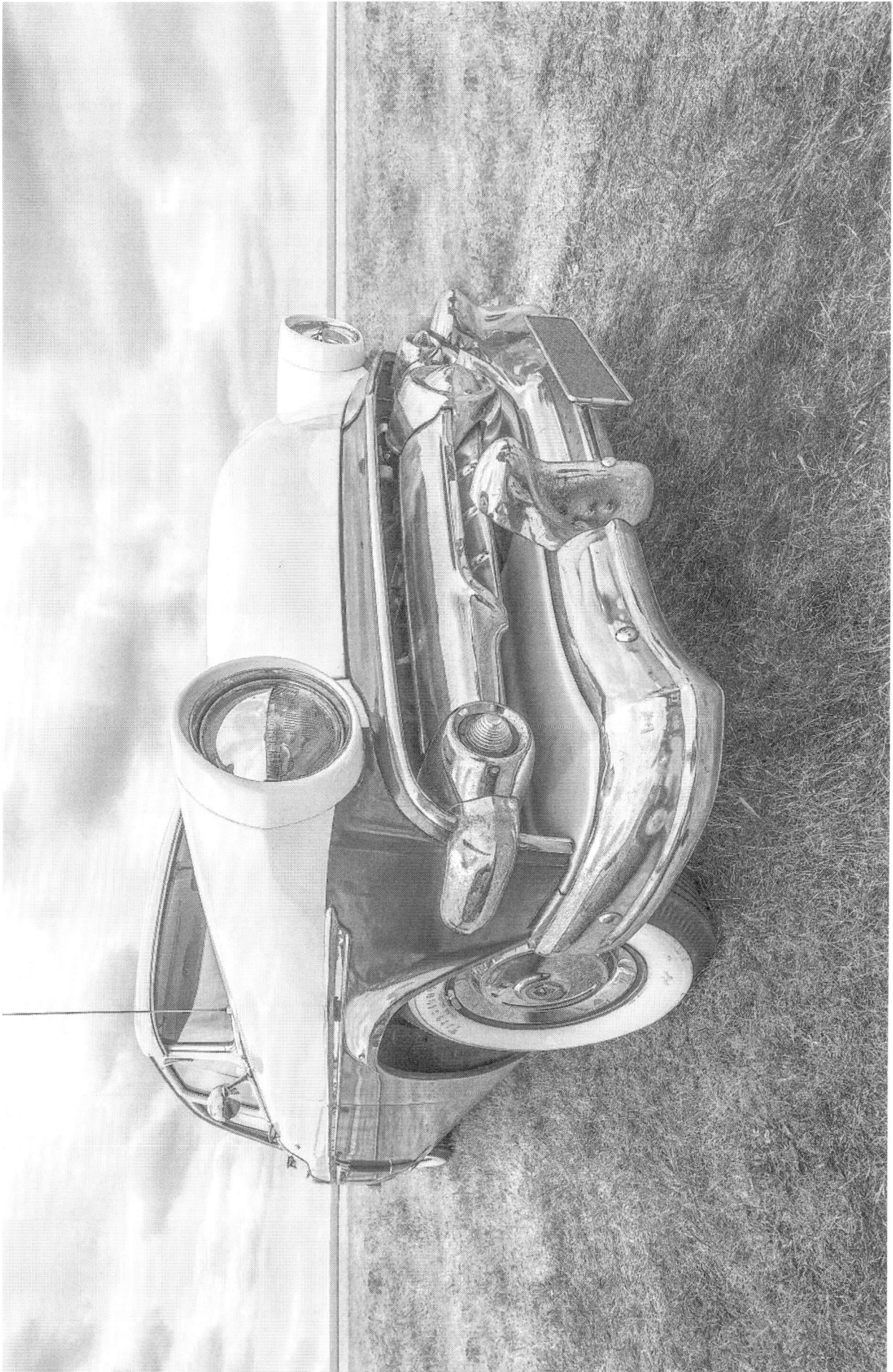

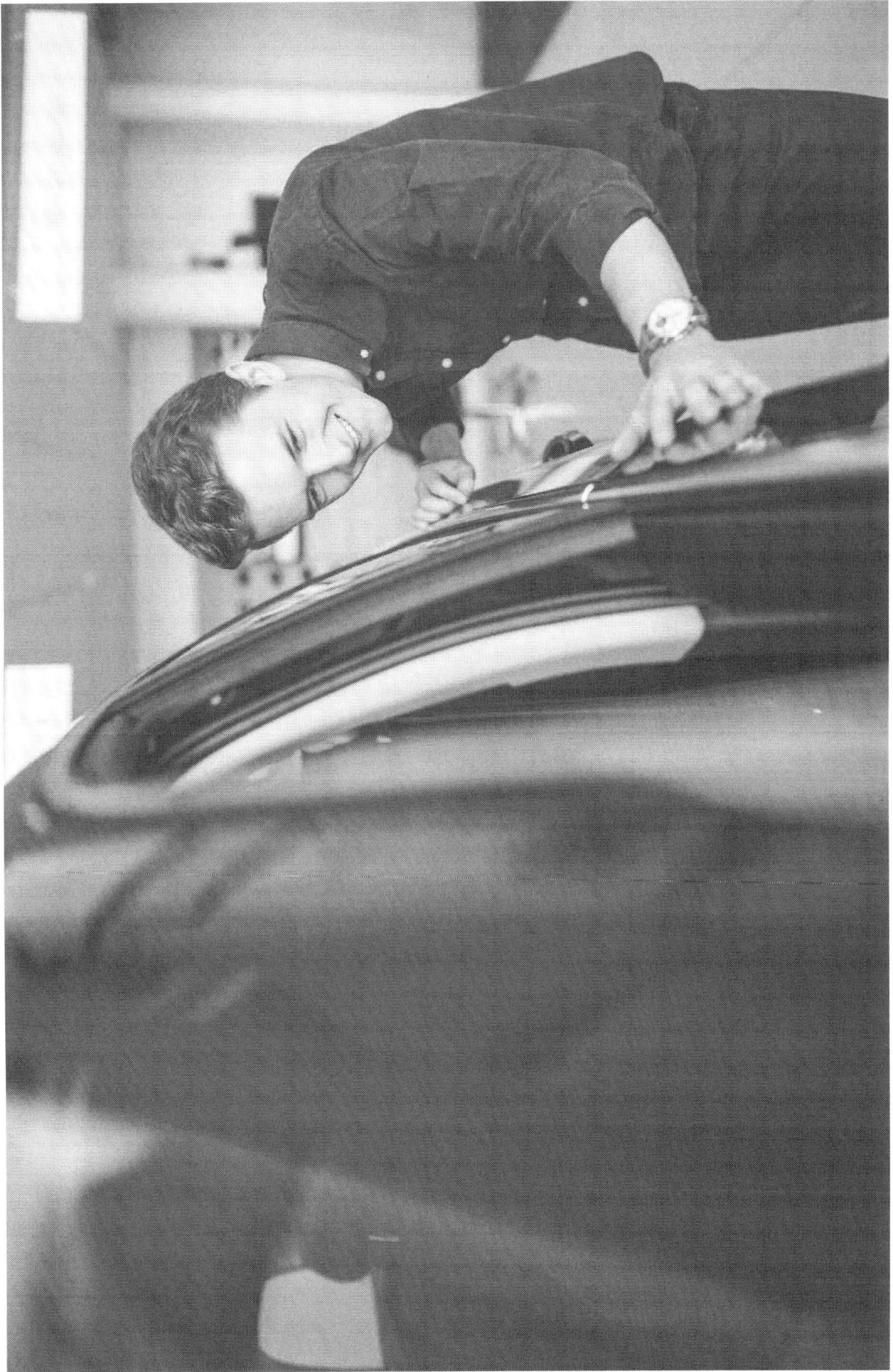

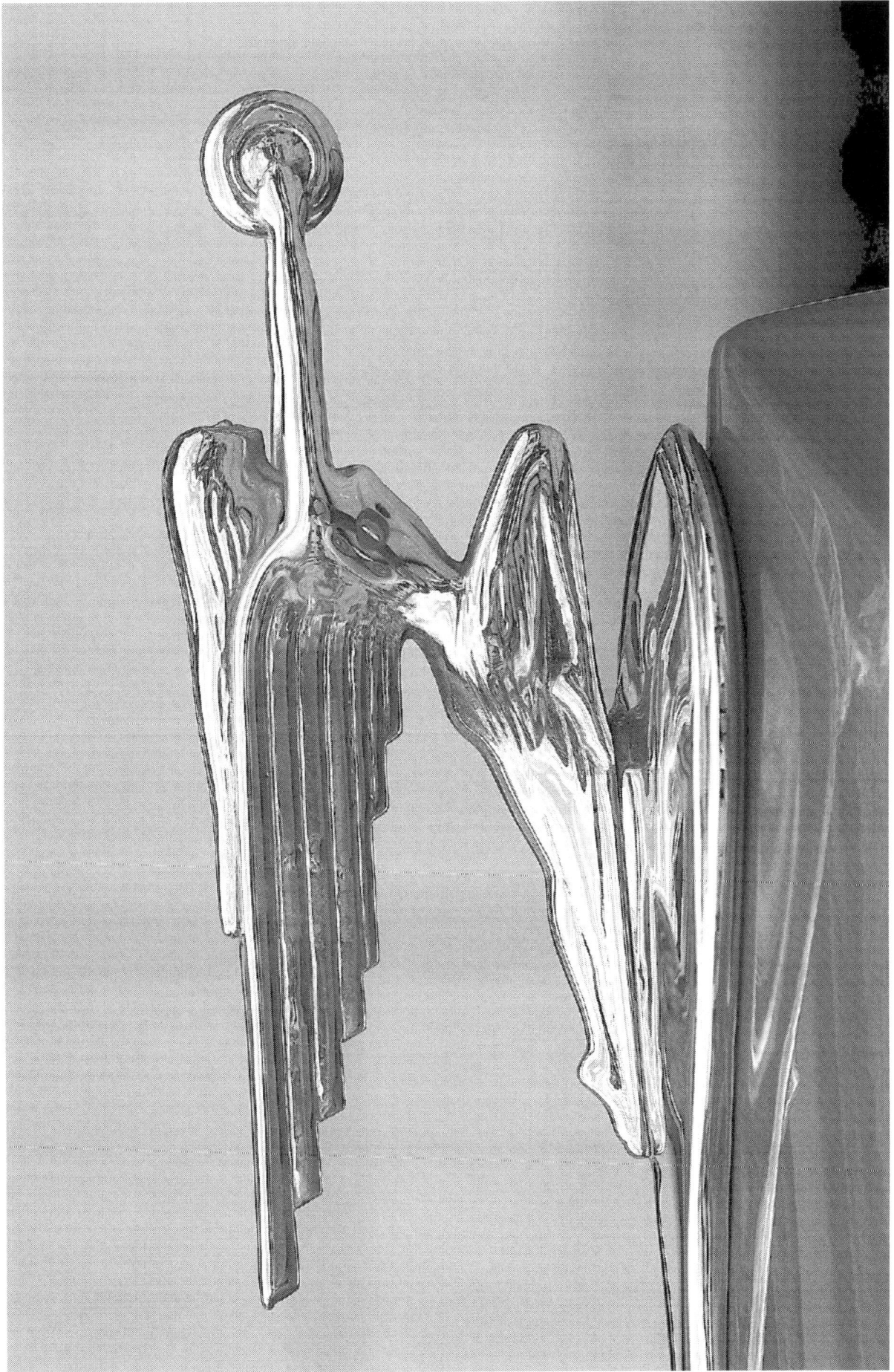

neue B-Klasse.
tify nothing

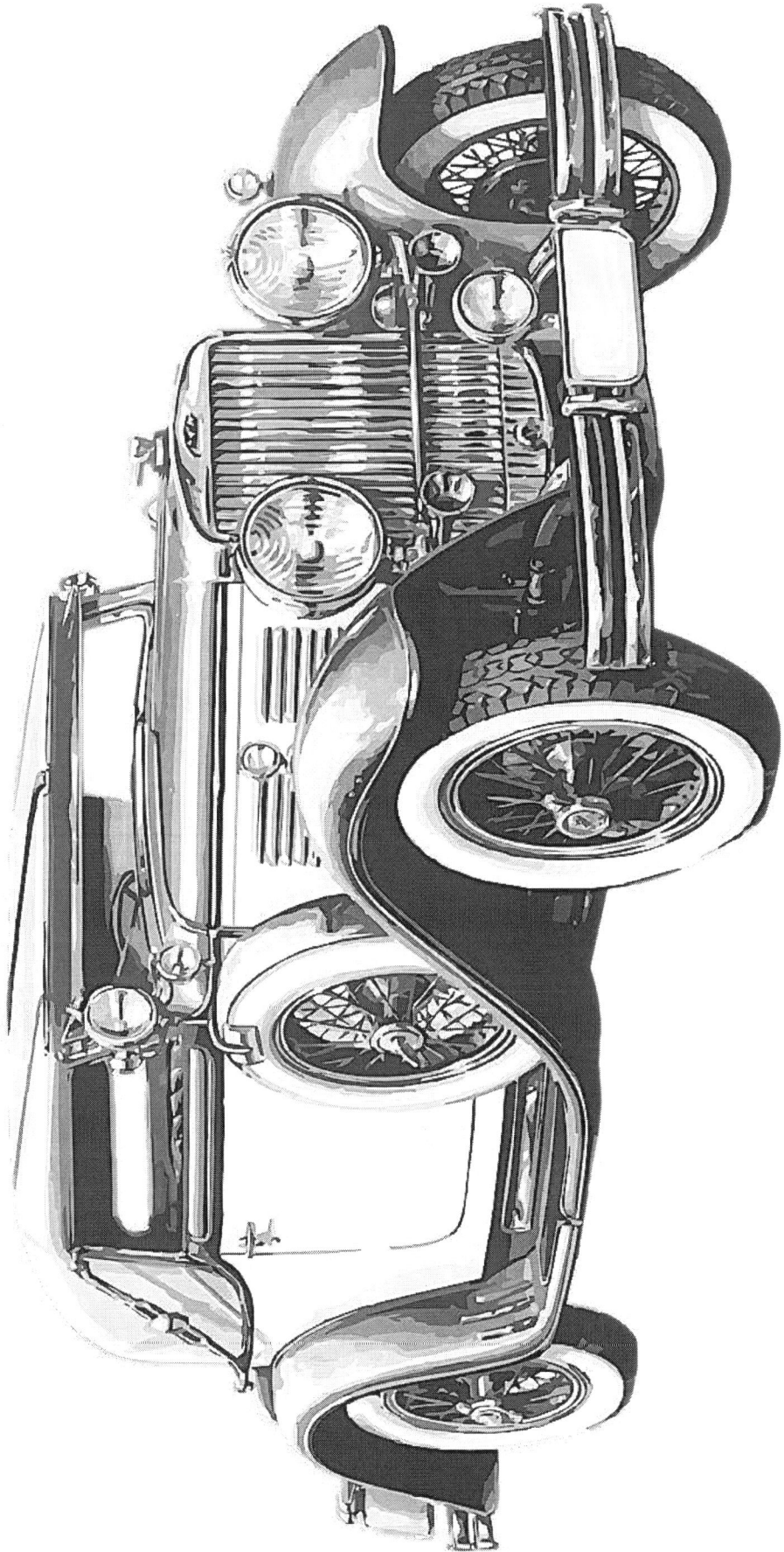

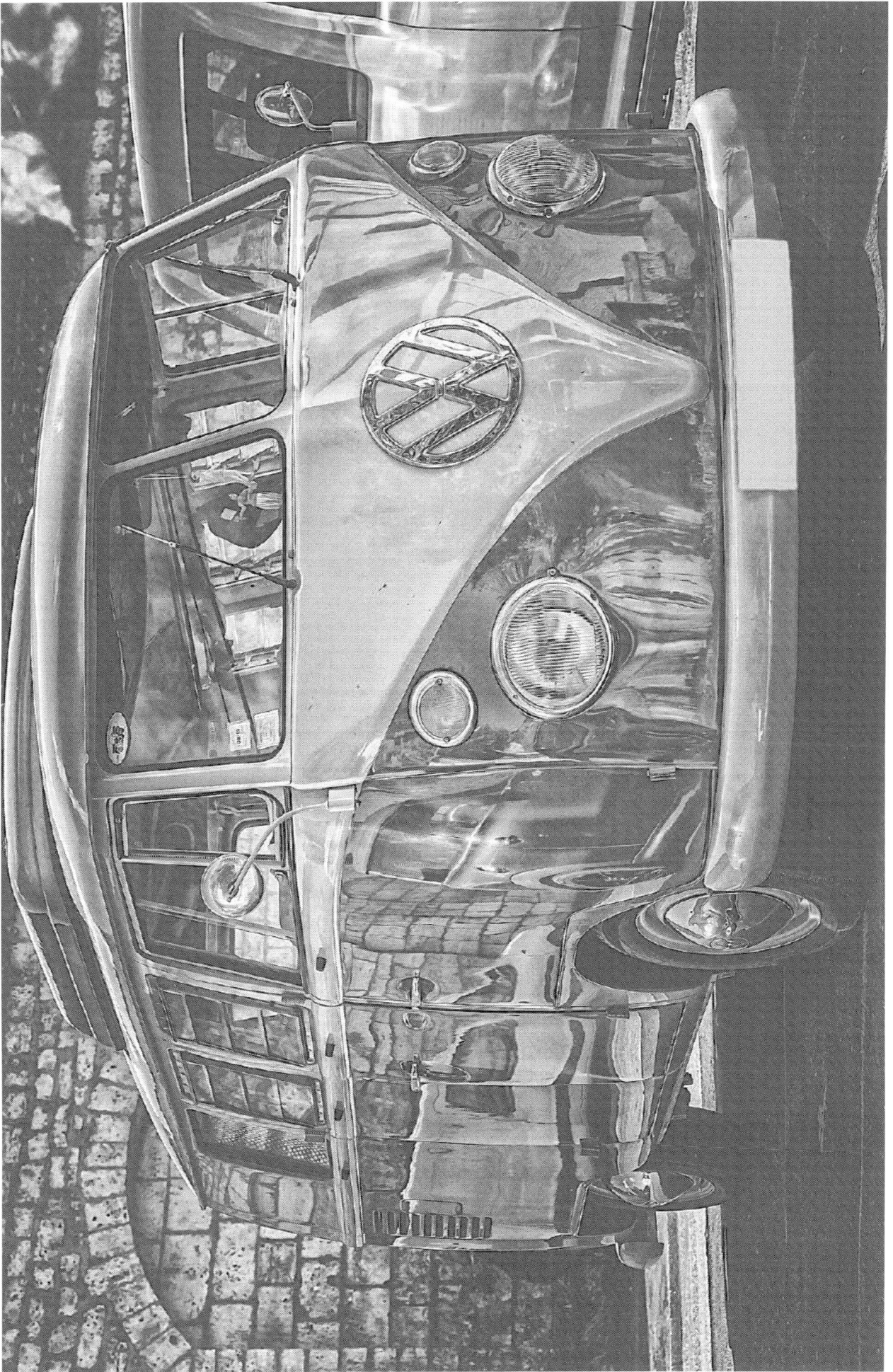